DESSERT FONDUES

SANDRA RUDLOFF

BRISTOL PUBLISHING ENTERPRISES
Hayward, California

A **nitty gritty**® cookbook

ISBN 1-55867-322-9

Cover design: Frank J. Paredes
Cover photography: John Benson
Food stylist: Randy Mon
Illustrations: Caryn Leschen

CONTENTS

AN INTRODUCTION TO DESSERT FONDUE

Many think of fondue as a winter dessert. But think of how wonderful a peanut butter fondue on fresh apples would be in the fall, or a light lemon fondue with strawberries and angel food cake would be in the summer. Change your traditional Easter menu by finishing with a creamy white chocolate fondue and dip in brownie bites or chocolate cookies.

A BRIEF HISTORY OF FONDUE

Almost all food historians agree that fondue was created in Switzerland in the 1800s. It was considered peasant food, as farmers or servants would use what they had on hand, usually hardened cheese and stale bread. Many noble travelers would pass through Switzerland on their way between Germany, France and Italy. Back then, the visiting servants ate with the house servants and learned new recipes from each other.

Fondue made its way out of Switzerland and to the rest of the world in the mid-twentieth century. In the late 1990s, fondue enjoyed a resurgence, and once again fondue is a fun way to entertain. Fondue pots, both electric and Sterno-heated, are readily available everywhere (if you no longer have your harvest gold pot from the '70s!).

FONDUES AND FONDON'TS

Since a group of people are sharing a fondue, there are a few basic guidelines to follow. For health reasons, suggest that your guests select assorted dippers from a tray and place them on their own plates. Each guest can then spear a dipper with the fondue fork and dip into the fondue once, twirling the fork. (Remember, no double dipping!) You can also provide separate forks to be used for eating, so your guests are not eating with the fondue forks they use to dip back into the pot. Many people think that they should swirl their dippers around and around the pot. This will cause your dipper to break up. After removing the dipper from the pot, twirl the food over the pot to allow any excess to drip back in the pot.

I've tried a few different types of fondue pots, and I think electric pots are the best. The heat is evenly distributed on the bottom, and can be adjusted from very low to very hot. You can both cook and serve most fondues this way. If you use a fondue pot heated with a candle or Sterno pot, be aware that the concentrated heat source may cause the center of your fondue to burn. These pots will rarely attain a high enough temperature to reach a simmer, much less a boil, so they're not the best for cooking, but are a good idea for serving chocolate fondues, which can seize up and become a clumpy mess if heated too high, and are best kept over very low heat. Conversely, caramel or toffee fondues initially need higher heat to melt the sugar. Although you can cook the mixture in an electric fondue pot, it's easier to cook these fondues in a heavy pan on your stove, and then transfer them to the fondue pot.

If your fondue gets too thick, add more of the base liquid (cream, half-and-half, etc.) and not more liquor, if used. Fruit-based fondues containing cornstarch must boil for the cornstarch to do its thickening magic.

Most fondue pots (and these recipes) are designed to serve six to eight people for dessert — the perfect amount for a family gathering or small dinner party. For a larger group, why not have a fondue potluck? Have one or two guests bring their own pots, assign an array of dippers for the other guests to bring, and provide a selection of chocolate-, fruit- and cream-based fondues. Dig in and watch the conversation flow around the table!

FONDUE FOLKLORE

If a lady loses her dipper in the pot, she is supposed to kiss all the men at the table. However, if a man loses his dipper, he has to buy a bottle of wine for the table.

NOTES ON KEY INGREDIENTS

Six ounces of chocolate (chips or finely chopped) equals 1 measuring cup; one pound of chopped chocolate (or chips) equals about $2^2/_3$ cups.

If liquor of any kind is brought to a boil, the alcohol content will be almost completely cooked off. If liquor is not boiled, the alcohol content remains. Keep this in mind when serving fondue containing liquor to those who may be sensitive to alcohol, especially children.

Standard dippers include chunks of angel food or pound cake, fresh strawberries, banana pieces or marshmallows. But you're really only limited by your imagination. Try pretzel rods, apple or pear wedges, mango or melon wedges, graham crackers, or even candy canes. For the best made-to-order dippers, see the *Dippers* chapter, page 82.

CHOCOLATE FONDUES

9   Classic Chocolate Fondue
10   Chocolate Deluxe Fondue
11   Mexican Chocolate Fondue
12   Aztec Chocolate Fondue
13   Chocolate Raspberry Fondue
14   Chocolate Grand Marnier Fondue
15   Chocolate Orange Fondue
16   Chocolate Rum Fondue
17   Irish Cream Chocolate Fondue
18   Whiskey Chocolate Fondue
19   Kahlúa Chocolate Fondue
20   Chocolate Almond Liqueur Fondue
21   Chocolate Mint Fondue
22   Chocolate Caramel Fondue
23   Chocolate Mocha Fondue

THE INCREDIBLE VARIETY OF CHOCOLATE FONDUES

From milk chocolate to bittersweet, from kid-friendly to sophisticated, chocolate fondues can please just about everyone. This section contains recipes based on milk, dark, semisweet, bittersweet and white chocolates. Many people have strong preferences for the types of chocolate they enjoy. If you don't like bittersweet chocolate, try the recipe using milk chocolate. Don't avoid the recipe because you don't enjoy a particular type of chocolate!

Use the best quality chocolate you can find. A rich, luxurious chocolate bar tastes better than store-brand baking chocolate chips, and your fondue will taste better also. One exception to this rule: use white chocolate baking chips when white chocolate is needed. Real white chocolate can easily separate when heated and will ruin your fondue.

Feel free to adjust the liquid in these recipes. Most will have a texture that will easily coat your dippers, but if you prefer a thicker fondue, decrease the liquid by a few tablespoons.

Low heat is essential when working with solid chocolate. (Cocoa powder is the exception here, as it can take the heat.) Chocolate will seize up into a solid mass if heated at too high a temperature. Melt chocolate alone or with butter on the stove or over a double boiler over very low heat; or melt chopped chocolate in a bowl in the microwave on high for 30 seconds at a time, stirring frequently; or add chopped chocolate to hot cream over low heat (or off heat). Any of these methods, if watched carefully, will ensure perfect melting. When preparing chocolate fondue in an electric fondue pot, keep the thermostat set on low. Remember, use low heat, stir often, and your chocolate fondue will be a creamy delight.

CLASSIC CHOCOLATE FONDUE

This is a family favorite. You can make this fondue kid-friendly by using milk choco-late and serving favorite dippers like marshmallows, Ultimate Krispie Treats, *page 99, or cookies. For adults, try dark or bittersweet choco-late and dippers of fresh straw-berries, raspberries and mixed nuts.*

1 cup heavy cream
1 lb. milk, dark or bittersweet
   chocolate, chopped
1 tsp. vanilla extract

In a saucepan or fondue pot, heat cream over low heat until very warm. Add chocolate and stir constantly over low heat until smooth. Do not boil. Remove from heat and add vanilla. Stir until well mixed. Keep over low heat when serving.

CHOCOLATE DELUXE FONDUE

Probably the richest of all the chocolate fondues, this one is best served with simple dippers like fresh strawberries or Sour Cream Pound Cake, *page 108.*

2 cups (12 oz.) semisweet chocolate chips
1 can (14 oz.) sweetened condensed milk
1 cup half-and-half
$1/4$ cup ($1/2$ stick) butter
1 tsp. vanilla extract

In a saucepan or fondue pot, combine chocolate chips, sweetened condensed milk, half-and-half, butter and vanilla. Stir over low heat until morsels and butter are melted and mixture is smooth. Do not boil. Keep over low heat when serving.

MEXICAN CHOCOLATE FONDUE

Chocolate and cinnamon make a unique fondue that is delicious after a Mexican meal, and chocolate is often flavored with cinnamon in Mexico.

1 cup half-and-half
$1/2$ tsp. cinnamon
1 lb. dark or bittersweet chocolate, chopped
1 tbs. dark rum

In a saucepan or fondue pot, heat half-and-half and cinnamon over low heat until mixture reaches a simmer. Simmer for 5 minutes to allow the cinnamon to flavor the cream. Add chocolate and stir constantly over low heat until smooth. Do not boil. Add rum and stir until well mixed. Keep over low heat when serving.

AZTEC CHOCOLATE FONDUE

Serves 6–8

Inspired by the movie "Chocolat," this is similar to Mexican Chocolate Fondue, page 11, but it has a subtle and surprising kick of heat at the end!

1 cup half-and-half
1/2 tsp. cinnamon
1/4 tsp. ground allspice
1/4 tsp. ground cloves
1/2 tsp. hot red pepper flakes
1 lb. dark or bittersweet chocolate, chopped

In a saucepan or fondue pot, heat half-and-half, cinnamon, allspice and hot red pepper flakes over low heat until very warm. Simmer for 10 minutes. Strain cream mixture to remove hot red pepper flakes. Return cream mixture to pot, add chocolate and stir constantly over low heat until smooth. Do not boil. Keep over low heat when serving.

CHOCOLATE RASPBERRY FONDUE

I like using bittersweet chocolate to offset the sweetness of the liquor. Using fresh raspberries as a dipper makes this even more spectacular.

$1/2$ cup half-and-half
1 lb. bittersweet or dark chocolate, chopped
$3/4$ cup framboise (raspberry brandy)

In a saucepan or fondue pot, heat half-and-half over low heat until very warm. Add chocolate and stir constantly over low heat until smooth. Do not boil. Remove from heat and add framboise. Stir until well mixed. Keep over low heat when serving.

CHOCOLATE GRAND MARNIER FONDUE

This is a special fondue to serve after an elegant dinner. With the addition of freshly squeezed orange juice and orange zest, this fondue has an intense orange flavor.

1 orange
$1/2$ cup heavy cream
$1/2$ lb. bittersweet or semisweet chocolate, chopped
$1/3$ cup Grand Marnier (orange liqueur)

Grate zest from the orange, making sure to not get any white pith. Reserve orange. Place zest and cream in a small saucepan or fondue pot and bring to a simmer over low heat. Simmer cream for a minute or so, then remove from heat and set aside to steep a few more minutes.

Meanwhile, squeeze the orange. Strain juice and set aside. Add chocolate to cream mixture, place over low heat and stir until chocolate has melted and mixture is smooth. Remove from heat to add orange juice and Grand Marnier. Keep over low heat when serving.

CHOCOLATE ORANGE FONDUE

Serves 6–8

If you like the flavor of those chocolate "oranges," you'll love this fondue. This is similar to Chocolate Grand Marnier Fondue, page *14, but without the alcohol.*

1 cup half-and-half
grated zest of 1 large orange
1 lb. milk chocolate, chopped

In a saucepan or fondue pot, heat half-and-half and orange zest over low heat until mixture reaches a simmer. Simmer for 10 minutes, stirring frequently, to allow the orange zest to flavor the half-and-half. Add chocolate and stir constantly over low heat until smooth. Do not boil. Keep over low heat when serving.

CHOCOLATE RUM FONDUE

I like to use spiced rum in this fondue, but you can use regular light or dark rum, or even a flavored rum.

$3/4$ cup heavy cream
1 lb. milk chocolate, chopped
$1/4$ cup spiced rum

In a saucepan or fondue pot, heat cream over low heat until very warm. Add chocolate and stir constantly over low heat until smooth. Do not boil. Remove from heat and add rum. Stir until well mixed. Keep over low heat when serving.

IRISH CREAM CHOCOLATE FONDUE

The Irish Cream liqueur makes this one of my favorite adults-only fondues. I love this in the winter — it makes me think of Christmas.

$^1/_2$ cup heavy cream
1 lb. milk chocolate, chopped
$^3/_4$ cup Irish Cream liqueur

In a saucepan or fondue pot, heat cream over low heat until very warm. Add chocolate and stir constantly over low heat until smooth. Do not boil. Remove from heat to add Irish Cream. Stir until well mixed. Keep over low heat when serving.

WHISKEY CHOCOLATE FONDUE

The flavors of chocolate and whiskey go surprisingly well together. Try after some barbecue for an unforgettable meal.

1 cup heavy cream
6 oz. milk chocolate, chopped
6 oz. dark or bittersweet chocolate, chopped
$1/4$ cup whiskey or bourbon

In a saucepan or fondue pot, heat cream over low heat until very warm. Add milk and dark chocolates and stir constantly over low heat until smooth. Do not boil. Remove from heat to stir in whiskey. Keep over low heat when serving.

KAHLÚA CHOCOLATE FONDUE

You can use any coffee-flavored liqueur for this, to make a rich mocha fondue.

$1/2$ cup heavy cream
1 tbs. instant coffee granules
1 lb. semisweet or dark chocolate, chopped
$1/2$ cup Kahlúa or other coffee liqueur

In a saucepan or fondue pot, heat cream over low heat until very warm. Add instant coffee and stir until dissolved. Add chocolate and stir constantly over low heat until smooth. Do not boil. Remove from heat to add Kahlúa. Stir until well mixed. Keep over low heat when serving.

CHOCOLATE ALMOND LIQUEUR FONDUE

Serves 6–8

The almonds in this fondue add flavor as well as crunch. You can use chopped or slivered almonds here. I like to lightly toast the almonds in the oven before using.

3/4 cup heavy cream
1 lb. milk chocolate, chopped
1/4 cup amaretto or other almond liqueur
1/3 cup chopped almonds

In a saucepan or fondue pot, heat cream over low heat until very warm. Add chocolate and stir constantly over low heat until smooth. Do not boil. Remove from heat to add amaretto and almonds; stir until well mixed. Keep over low heat when serving.

almonds

CHOCOLATE MINT FONDUE

Warm fondue with the cool taste of mint, this can be served any time of year.

1 cup heavy cream
1 lb. milk chocolate, chopped
$\frac{1}{2}$ tsp. mint extract

In a saucepan or fondue pot, heat cream over low heat until very warm. Add chocolate and stir constantly over low heat until smooth. Do not boil. Add mint extract and stir until well mixed. Keep over low heat when serving.

mint

CHOCOLATE CARAMEL FONDUE

Serves 6–8

This is a very sweet fondue, so use dippers that aren't too sugary. Fresh fruits, and plain vanilla cookies and cakes are the best.

1 cup sugar
2 cups heavy cream
1 tsp. vanilla extract
$1/2$ lb. semisweet or dark chocolate, chopped

In a heavy medium saucepan, heat sugar over medium-high heat until sugar is melted. Continue to cook until sugar is light brown in color, about 3 to 4 minutes. Watch carefully, as caramel can go from brown to burned very quickly.

Remove from heat and carefully add cream and vanilla; mixture will emit steam and may foam up. Stir until well mixed. Return to medium heat and cook for another 5 to 10 minutes, until mixture is thick. Reduce heat to low and add chocolate, stirring constantly to melt chocolate. Transfer to fondue pot. Keep over low heat when serving.

CHOCOLATE MOCHA FONDUE

Coffee and chocolate are natural partners, and this fondue can be adjusted to sat-isfy the coffee addict in your party. If you like a stronger coffee flavor, increase the ground coffee to $1/2$ cup.

1 cup half-and-half
$1/4$ cup ground coffee
1 lb. milk or dark chocolate, chopped

In a saucepan or fondue pot, heat cream and coffee over low heat until mixture reaches a simmer. Simmer for 10 minutes. Pour coffee-cream mixture through a strain-er lined with a coffee filter. Return cream to pot. Add chocolate and stir constantly over low heat until smooth. Do not boil. Keep over low heat when serving.

LOW FAT CHOCOLATE FONDUE

This is as good as any of the fondues using heavy cream and chocolate. The evaporated milk helps make it smooth. It will remind you of very rich hot cocoa.

$1/2$ cup unsweetened cocoa powder
1 cup sugar
1 tbs. cornstarch
12 oz. fat-free evaporated milk
1 tsp. vanilla extract

Mix cocoa powder, sugar and cornstarch together in a saucepan off heat, until well combined and free of lumps. Stir in evaporated milk and vanilla until well mixed. Warm over low heat, stirring constantly, until sugar has dissolved and mixture is smooth. Transfer to a fondue pot for serving.

CHOCOLATE PEANUT BUTTER FONDUE

Serves 6–8

Think of a melted peanut butter cup! If you use a peanut butter that is "natural style," with no added ingredients, your fondue will be much more flavorful.

1⅓ cups heavy cream
1 cup natural style peanut butter
1 lb. milk or semisweet chocolate, chopped

In a saucepan or fondue pot, heat cream and peanut butter over low heat until very warm and well combined. Add chocolate and stir constantly over low heat until smooth. Do not boil. Keep over low heat when serving.

CHOCOLATE S'MORES FONDUE

Serves 4–6

To be able to taste all the flavors in this fondue, you don't need a lot of chocolate. Graham crackers are family-favorite dippers. You may need to increase the amount of half-and-half, depending on which brand of marshmallow crème you use. Just be sure to add it once you've added the chocolate and it has melted completely.

$1/3$ cup half-and-half
1 jar (7 oz.) marshmallow crème
6 oz. milk chocolate, chopped

In a saucepan or fondue pot, heat half-and-half over low heat until very warm. Add marshmallow crème and stir constantly over low heat until smooth. Add chocolate and stir until melted and well mixed. Do not boil. Keep over low heat when serving.

CHOCOLATE CHEESECAKE FONDUE

Chocolate takes a lesser role to the cream cheese in this fondue. This rich dessert should be served after a lighter meal.

1$\frac{1}{4}$ cups half-and-half
8 oz. cream cheese, cubed
6 oz. dark chocolate, chopped

In a saucepan or fondue pot, heat cream over low heat until very warm. Add cream cheese and stir until melted. Add chocolate and stir constantly over low heat until smooth. Do not boil. Keep over low heat when serving.

CHOCOLATE RASPBERRY CHEESECAKE FONDUE

Serves 6–8

Another very rich fondue, it is best served after a lighter meal.

1/2 cup milk
1/2 cup seedless raspberry preserves
1 cup (6 oz.) semisweet chocolate chips
6 oz. cream cheese, cubed

In a saucepan or fondue pot, heat milk and preserves over low heat. When very warm, add chocolate and cream cheese. Stir until melted and smooth. Do not boil. Keep over low heat when serving.

twirl your fork!

SWISS CHOCOLATE FONDUE

Reportedly, in the 1950s, Chef Konrad Egli created the original recipe for chocolate fondue at New York's Chalet Swiss Restaurant (no longer in business). Use about 9 ounces of good quality milk chocolate if you can't find Toblerone bars.

3 bars (3 oz. each) Toblerone chocolate
$\frac{1}{2}$ cup light or heavy cream
2 tbs. Cointreau (orange liqueur)

Break Toblerone into separate triangular pieces; set aside. In a saucepan or fondue pot, heat cream over low heat until very warm. Add chocolate and stir constantly over low heat until smooth. Do not boil. Add Cointreau and stir until well mixed. Keep over low heat when serving.

CHOCOLATE YOGURT FONDUE

Yogurt (low fat or fat-free are fine) adds a subtle tang that balances the richness of the chocolate and rum.

1 lb. semisweet chocolate, chopped
2 tbs. dark rum
1 tbs. butter
1 container (8 oz.) plain or vanilla yogurt, at room temperature

In a saucepan or fondue pot, combine chocolate, rum and butter. Place over low heat and warm, stirring constantly, just until chocolate has melted and mixture is smooth. Do not boil. Remove from heat and stir in yogurt. Keep over low heat when serving.

CHOCOLATE SOUR CREAM FONDUE

The sour cream makes this fondue taste like warm chocolate cheesecake.

$1/3$ cup half-and-half
1 lb. milk chocolate, chopped
1 tsp. instant coffee granules
$2/3$ cup sour cream

In a saucepan or fondue pot, heat half-and-half over low heat. Add chocolate and instant coffee; stir until melted and smooth. Do not boil. Add sour cream and stir until mixture is well blended. Keep over low heat when serving.

CHOCOLATE MALT FONDUE

A throwback to the flavors of an old-fashioned chocolate malt milkshake, this fondue is delicious with graham crackers or pound cake dippers.

1 cup heavy cream
12 oz. milk chocolate, chopped
6 tbs. malted milk powder

In a saucepan or fondue pot, heat cream over low heat until very warm. Add chocolate and stir constantly over low heat until smooth. Do not boil. Add malted milk powder and stir until well mixed. Keep over low heat when serving.

SUPER EASY "FONDUE"

If you want to make fondue in an instant, this is for you. Not as rich as a standard chocolate fondue, it's the perfect choice if you're in a time crunch, or if you just don't feel like cooking but want a yummy dessert.

1 bottle (19 oz.) fudge ice cream topping
$^{1}/_{4}$ cup heavy cream

In a saucepan or fondue pot, combine fudge topping and cream until smooth. Warm mixture over low heat, stirring frequently. Serve over low heat.

MICROWAVE DIRECTIONS

Combine fudge topping and cream in a microwave-safe bowl. Heat on medium power for 30 seconds. Stir. Continue to heat in 30-second increments, on medium power, until desired consistency has been reached, stirring every 30 seconds. Transfer to a fondue pot for serving.

SUPER FUDGY FONDUE

This thick, rich fondue is best with simple dippers, so that you can enjoy the buttery taste.

$^1/_2$ cup (1 stick) butter
$^1/_2$ cup unsweetened cocoa powder
$^3/_4$ cup sugar
$^1/_2$ cup evaporated milk
1 tsp. vanilla extract

In a saucepan or fondue pot, melt butter over low heat. In a small bowl, combine cocoa powder and sugar. Add cocoa mixture to butter and stir constantly over low heat until smooth. Add evaporated milk and stir until well mixed. Stir in vanilla. Keep over low heat when serving.

CHOCOLATE HONEY FONDUE

Honey and chocolate are not normally paired up in cooking, but are heavenly together in this fondue. Try this with banana slices.

$^1/_2$ cup heavy cream
$^1/_4$ cup honey
8 oz. semisweet chocolate, chopped

In a saucepan or fondue pot, heat cream over low heat until very warm. Add honey and stir until mixed. Add chocolate and stir until melted and well combined. Do not boil. Keep over low heat when serving.

FRANGELICO FONDUE

Frangelico, a hazelnut liqueur, enhances the nutty flavor of this dessert.

$1/2$ cup (1 stick) butter
$1/2$ cup granulated sugar
$1/2$ cup light brown sugar, packed
$1/4$ cup unsweetened cocoa powder
$1 1/4$ cups heavy cream
$1/4$ cup Frangelico (hazelnut liqueur)
$1/4$ cup chopped hazelnuts or almonds

In a saucepan or fondue pot, melt butter over medium heat. Add sugars and cocoa powder and stir until mixed. Add cream and stir until mixture is well blended. Cook over medium heat for about 8 to 10 minutes. Remove from heat to add Frangelico and nuts. Keep over low heat when serving.

CHOCOLATE CARAMEL RASPBERRY FONDUE

Serves 6–8

Impress your guests with this fabulous combination of flavors. Plain dippers, such as pound cake or Buttery Shortbread, *page 105, are best with this complex fondue.*

1 can (12 oz.) evaporated milk
$1/2$ cup (1 stick) butter
$1/2$ cup seedless raspberry preserves
1 pkg. (14 oz.) caramels, unwrapped
2 cups (12 oz.) semisweet chocolate chips

In a saucepan or fondue pot, heat evaporated milk and butter over medium heat. When milk is very warm and butter has melted, reduce heat to low and add raspberry preserves, caramels and chocolate and stir until melted and smooth. Do not boil. Keep over low heat when serving.

SMOOTH CHOCOLATE ALMOND FONDUE

Almond butter, similar to peanut butter, can often be found in the natural foods section of your grocery store, and always in health food stores.

1¼ cups heavy cream
1 cup almond butter
1 tsp. almond extract
1 lb. semisweet chocolate, chopped

In a saucepan or fondue pot, heat cream and almond butter over low heat until very warm. Add extract and chocolate and stir constantly over low heat until smooth. Do not boil. Keep over low heat when serving.

QUICK CHOCOLATE HAZELNUT FONDUE

This fondue is a bit of a cheat since it uses Nutella, the chocolate-hazelnut spread, as a base. It is easy and wonderful and can be made kid-friendly by omitting the liqueur.

2 cups Nutella spread
1 1/2 cups heavy cream
1/4 cup Frangelico hazelnut liqueur

Combine Nutella, cream and Frangelico in a saucepan or fondue pot and heat over low heat until very warm.

CHOCOLATE PECAN FONDUE

This is a cross between a pecan pie and chocolate fondue. Toast the pecans before adding to the fondue, if you wish, for a more pronounced flavor.

2/3 cup light or dark corn syrup
1/2 cup heavy cream
1 pkg. (8 oz.) semisweet chocolate chips
1 cup chopped pecans

In a saucepan or fondue pot, mix together corn syrup and cream. Bring to a boil over medium heat. Remove from heat, add chocolate and stir until melted. Stir in pecans. Keep over low heat when serving.

WHITE CHOCOLATE FONDUE

Serves 6–8

This simple fondue is the perfect coating for fresh fruits such as berries, pineapple or pears.

1 cup heavy cream
1 lb. white chocolate baking chips
2 tbs. Kirsch (cherry brandy)

In a saucepan or fondue pot, heat cream over low heat until very warm. Add chocolate and stir constantly over low heat until smooth. Do not boil. Add Kirsch and stir to combine. Keep over low heat when serving.

WHITE CHOCOLATE BANANA FONDUE

Think of this as a warm banana cream pie! Vanilla wafers go well with this as a dipper. For a completely different taste, try using milk or dark chocolate instead of white chocolate.

1 cup heavy cream
1 lb. white chocolate baking chips
1 tsp. banana extract, or more to taste

In a saucepan or fondue pot, heat cream over low heat until very warm. Add white chocolate and stir constantly over low heat until smooth. Do not boil. Stir in extract. Keep over low heat when serving.

WHITE CHOCOLATE PEPPERMINT FONDUE

This fondue is perfect for the holidays, when you may have some spare candy canes. Brownie Cookies, *page 96, are wonderful dippers.*

1 cup heavy cream
1 cup chopped candy canes (about 12 candy canes)
1 lb. white chocolate baking chips

In a saucepan or fondue pot, heat cream over low heat until very warm. Add chopped candy canes and stir until candy is melted. Add white chocolate and stir constantly over low heat until smooth. Do not boil. Keep over low heat when serving.

CAFFE LATTE FONDUE

This fondue uses instant coffee and white chocolate to make a smooth and sweet coffee dip. Chocolate-flavored dippers are my favorite with this fondue.

1 cup half-and-half
$1/4$ cup instant coffee granules
1 lb. white chocolate baking chips

In a saucepan or fondue pot, heat cream and instant coffee over medium low heat until very warm. Simmer for 10 minutes. Add white chocolate and stir constantly over low heat until smooth. Do not boil. Keep over low heat when serving.

BRANDY ALEXANDER FONDUE

This is a fondue version of the delicious after-dinner drink of the same name.

$1/2$ cup half-and-half
1 lb. white chocolate baking chips
$1/4$ cup brandy
$1/4$ cup crème de cacao (chocolate liqueur)

In a saucepan or fondue pot, heat half-and-half over low heat until very warm. Add white chocolate and stir until melted. Do not boil. Remove from heat to stir in brandy and crème de cacao until well mixed. Keep over low heat when serving.

FRUIT AND CREAMY FONDUES

64	Praline Fondue
65	Peppermint Fondue
66	Marshmallow Fondue
67	Irish Cream Fondue
68	Amaretto Mascarpone Cheese Fondue
69	Coconut Fondue
70	Cranberry Raspberry Fondue
71	Hot Berry Fondue
72	Cherries Jubilee Fondue
73	Cherry Cranberry Fondue
74	Maple Cherry Fondue
75	Lemon Fondue
76	Rum Raisin Fondue
77	Creamy Rum Raisin Fondue
78	Apricot Cream Fondue
79	Orange Marmalade Fondue

When thinking of dessert fondues, most people think of chocolate. The fondues in this section are based other ingredients, including cream, fruit or liquor. They are a fun change of pace from chocolate fondues and most can be served any time of year.

Fruit-based fondues, like the *Lemon Fondue,* page 75, *Cherry Cranberry Fondue,* page 73, or *Hot Berry Fondue,* page 71, are light and refreshing, perfect after a rich meal. Others, such as *Peanut Butter Fondue,* page 50, or *Marshmallow Fondue,* page 66, are fun and surprising choices for children's parties. And some, like *Praline Fondue,* page 64, are decadent indulgences.

When planning your next fondue get-together, think out of the box and try one — or more — of these unexpected delights.

PEANUT BUTTER HONEY FONDUE

Sweet and smooth, this is wonderful with bananas and pound cake. Use creamy or chunky-style peanut butter — both are delicious. Natural, additive-free peanut butter will provide the best flavor, whichever style you choose. Use ²/₃ cup of turbinado (raw) sugar instead of honey if you're not a honey fan.

1 cup natural style peanut butter
3/4 cup heavy cream
1/2 cup honey

Combine peanut butter, cream and honey in a saucepan or fondue pot. Heat over low heat until very warm and smooth, stirring constantly. Keep over low heat when serving.

PEANUT BUTTER FONDUE

After chocolate, the peanut butter fondues were the most requested from my taste testers. Maybe because kids love it as much as the adults, or maybe because the adults never outgrew it.

2 cups natural style chunky peanut butter
1 can (5⅓ oz.) evaporated milk
1 cup light brown sugar, packed
¼ cup (½ stick) butter

In a fondue pot or small saucepan, mix together peanut butter, evaporated milk, brown sugar and butter and place over medium-low heat. Stir frequently until fondue is very warm, butter has melted and sugar has dissolved. Keep over low heat when serving.

CINNAMON FONDUE

Not only is this fondue delicious, the spicy aroma will fill your house. Apple wedges and Chocolate Biscotti Bites, *page 104, are fantastic accompaniments.*

²/₃ cup butter
1¹/₃ cups sugar
1 cup heavy cream
1¹/₄ tsp. cinnamon

In a saucepan or fondue pot, combine butter, sugar, cream and cinnamon. Warm over low heat until sugar has dissolved and butter has melted. Keep over low heat when serving.

RED HOT! CINNAMON FONDUE

If your kids like cinnamon candies, they will love this fondue. This ruby-red fondue is also perfect for a Valentine's Day dinner.

1 cup sugar
4 tsp. cornstarch
$1/_2$ cup water
$1/_2$ cup apple juice
1 cup red hot cinnamon candies

In a saucepan or fondue pot off heat, combine sugar and cornstarch until well blended. Add water, apple juice and candies. Warm over low heat until sugar has dissolved and candies are fully melted, stirring frequently. Keep over low heat when serving.

WINTER SPICE FONDUE

This fragrant fondue is perfect with apple wedges and Sour Cream Pound Cake, page *108, or* Nutty Biscotti, *page 100.*

$^2/_3$ cup sugar
3 tbs. cornstarch
$^1/_2$ tsp. cinnamon
$^1/_4$ tsp. ground cloves
$^1/_4$ tsp. ground allspice

$^1/_4$ tsp. ground ginger
2 cups whole milk (not low fat)
$^1/_4$ cup ($^1/_2$ stick) butter
$^1/_4$ tsp. vanilla extract

In a saucepan or fondue pot, combine sugar, cornstarch, cinnamon, cloves, allspice and ginger. Add milk and stir until well mixed. Bring to a boil over medium heat. Cook for 1 minute, stirring constantly, until smooth and thickened. Remove from heat and add butter and vanilla, stirring until butter is melted. Keep over low heat when serving.

PUMPKIN FONDUE

Serves 8–10

Instead of the traditional pumpkin pie this Thanksgiving, try this fondue.

1$\frac{1}{2}$ cups heavy cream
1 cup sugar
1 can (16 oz.) pumpkin puree
$\frac{1}{2}$ tsp. cinnamon
$\frac{1}{2}$ tsp. ground ginger
$\frac{1}{2}$ tsp. ground nutmeg
$\frac{1}{2}$ tsp. ground allspice
$\frac{1}{2}$ tsp. ground cloves

In a large fondue pot, warm cream and sugar over medium heat, stirring frequently, until sugar has dissolved. Add pumpkin, cinnamon, ginger, nutmeg, allspice and cloves and stir until combined. Continue to heat until fondue is thoroughly warmed and smooth.

HONEY FONDUE

Sweet and comforting, fragrant honey makes a versatile fondue. Lovely with fruit dippers, it's also perfect with cakes.

1/2 cup (1 stick) butter
1/2 cup honey
1 1/2 tbs. cornstarch
1/2 cup orange juice
1 cup heavy cream

In a fondue pot or small saucepan, heat butter and honey until mixture is very warm and butter is melted. In a small bowl, dissolve cornstarch in orange juice and add to butter mixture. Cook over low heat, stirring constantly, until very thick. Add cream and stir until smooth. Keep warm over low heat.

SIMPLY VANILLA FONDUE

Serves 6–8

This simple fondue, rich and full of vanilla flavor, is delicious with almost any dipper.

1 vanilla bean, split lengthwise
2 cups heavy cream
1 cup sugar
2 tbs. cornstarch
1 tsp. vanilla extract

Scrape seeds from vanilla bean into a fondue pot or saucepan. Add cream and stir to combine. In a small bowl, combine sugar and cornstarch. Stir well and add to cream. Bring mixture just to a boil over medium heat, stirring constantly. Add vanilla extract, reduce heat to low and simmer until thickened. Keep over low heat when serving.

CHEESECAKE FONDUE

This tastes like a warm slice of cheesecake. Strawberries and blueberries are my favorite dippers.

1 cup half-and-half
8 oz. cream cheese, cubed
1/4 cup sugar
1 tsp. grated lemon zest
2 tsp. freshly squeezed lemon juice
1 tsp. vanilla extract

In a saucepan or fondue pot, heat half-and-half over low heat until very warm. Add cream cheese to half-and-half, stirring until melted. Add sugar, lemon zest, lemon juice and vanilla. Stir until sugar has dissolved and fondue is smooth. Keep over low heat when serving.

BLACK WALNUT FONDUE

Maple and walnuts make delicious ice cream and an even better fondue. This is great when dipped with angel food cake. Use regular walnuts if black walnuts aren't available.

1 cup heavy cream
1 lb. white chocolate baking chips
1 tsp. maple flavoring
$^3/_4$ cup finely chopped black walnuts

In a saucepan or fondue pot, heat cream over low heat until very warm. Add white chocolate and stir until melted and smooth. Stir in maple flavoring and walnuts. Keep over low heat when serving.

BUTTERSCOTCH FONDUE

Another fondue on the sweeter side, butterscotch fondue is great after a light meal and should be served with lightly sweetened cakes and cookies, or fresh fruit.

1 cup brown sugar, packed
$1/4$ cup light corn syrup
$1/4$ cup ($1/2$ stick) butter
1 pinch salt
$1/2$ cup heavy cream, at room temperature
$1 1/2$ tsp. vanilla extract
2 tbs. dark rum, optional

In a heavy medium saucepan, combine brown sugar, corn syrup, butter and salt. Bring to a boil over medium heat, stirring frequently. Reduce heat and simmer for 12 minutes, stirring occasionally. Remove from heat and carefully stir in cream — mixture will emit steam and may foam up. Stir in vanilla and rum, if using. Keep over low heat when serving.

KIDS' FAVORITE BUTTERSCOTCH FONDUE

Serves 6–8

Served with apple slices, this fondue makes a nice after-school treat, and the kids can help to make it.

⅔ cup evaporated milk
2 cups butterscotch-flavored chips
1 jar (7 oz.) marshmallow crème

In a fondue pot or small saucepan, heat evaporated milk until very warm. Remove from heat and add butterscotch chips and marshmallow crème. Stir until chips are melted and mixture is smooth. Keep over low heat when serving.

TOFFEE FONDUE

Fondues on the sweeter side, such as this one, pair up best with fruits or nuts instead of baked goods. This is great with apples, pears, bananas or pecans.

$1/2$ cup (1 stick) butter
2 cups dark brown sugar, packed
1 cup white corn syrup
2 tbs. water
1 can (14 oz.) sweetened condensed milk
1 tsp. vanilla extract

In a fondue pot or small saucepan over medium heat, melt butter. Add brown sugar, corn syrup, water and condensed milk. Cook, stirring constantly, until mixture is thick and brown sugar has dissolved. Stir in vanilla. Keep over low heat when serving.

CARAMEL FONDUE

Apples and pears are the perfect dippers. Try serving chopped peanuts alongside and you can dip your apple pieces in the fondue and then into the nuts.

1 cup sugar
$1/4$ cup water
$2\frac{1}{2}$ cups heavy cream, room temperature
1 tsp. vanilla
$1/4$ cup brandy
2 tbs. butter

In a medium saucepan or fondue pot, combine sugar and water. Stir over low heat until all sugar dissolves. Increase heat to medium and boil without stirring until mixture is a deep amber color, occasionally brushing down sides of pan with a wet pastry brush, about 3 to 4 minutes. Watch carefully, as caramel can go from brown to burned very quickly. Remove from heat and carefully add cream and vanilla; mixture will emit steam and may foam up. Stir until well mixed. Return pan to stove over medium heat and cook, stirring, until sauce is thick and smooth, about 4 minutes. Carefully add brandy and cook 1 minute longer. Remove from heat and add butter. Stir until butter is melted. Keep over low heat when serving.

PRALINE FONDUE

You can use a pound of purchased pralines for this recipe instead of sugar and nuts.

1 cup sugar
1 cup almonds or pecans
1$\frac{1}{3}$ cups heavy cream
1 lb. white chocolate baking chips

To make praline, oil a cookie sheet; set aside. In a heavy small saucepan, heat sugar and almonds over medium-low heat until sugar is melted. Continue to cook until sugar is light brown in color, about 3 to 4 minutes. Watch carefully, as caramel can go from brown to burned very quickly. Pour at once onto prepared cookie sheet, then set aside to cool and harden for at least 15 minutes.

Break cooled praline into large chunks, then put into a food processor workbowl and pulse until chopped but not ground to a powder.

In a fondue pot or small saucepan, heat cream until very warm. Add white chocolate and stir until melted and smooth. Add praline pieces, stir to combine, and serve.

PEPPERMINT FONDUE

Pale pink or bright red? It's your choice. There's just a hint of mint, so once you have made the fondue, taste and adjust the peppermint flavor a drop at a time to your preference. This is lovely with Brownie Cookies, *page 96.*

2½ cups half-and-half
1 cup confectioner's sugar
2 tbs. flour

1 tbs. water
¼ tsp. peppermint extract, or to taste
1–2 drops red food coloring

In a fondue pot or small saucepan, mix together half-and-half and sugar and place over medium heat. Stir frequently until very warm and sugar is dissolved.

In a small bowl, blend flour with water into a smooth paste, add to half-and-half and continue to heat, stirring with a wire whisk, until fondue is thickened. Add peppermint extract and food coloring. Adjust mint flavor to taste. Keep over low heat when serving.

MARSHMALLOW FONDUE

It may be obvious, but graham crackers and chocolate pieces are required dippers!

1 can (14 oz.) sweetened condensed milk
1 jar (10 oz.) marshmallow crème
$\frac{1}{2}$ cup milk
1 teaspoon vanilla or almond extract

Combine condensed milk, marshmallow crème, milk and vanilla in a saucepan or fondue pot. Cook slowly over low heat until well blended and creamy. Keep over low heat when serving.

IRISH CREAM FONDUE

Serves 6–8

This grownups-only fondue is so-o-o good when dipped with chocolate cakes and cookies, such as Fudgy Nutty Cookies, *page 93.*

1/4 cup sugar
2 tbs. cornstarch
1 cup Irish Cream liqueur
1 cup heavy cream

In a saucepan or fondue pot off heat, combine sugar and cornstarch and stir until blended. Add Irish Cream and heavy cream and stir to mix well. Warm over low heat until sugar has dissolved and mixture is thickened. Keep over low heat when serving.

AMARETTO MASCARPONE CHEESE FONDUE

Mascarpone is a soft, rich Italian cheese similar to cream cheese and is used when making the dessert tiramisù. Serve this rich fondue with fruit.

1¹/₂ cups (about 12 oz.) mascarpone cheese
¹/₄ cup sugar
¹/₄ cup amaretto liqueur
¹/₂ tsp. cinnamon
¹/₂ tsp. ground nutmeg

In a medium saucepan or fondue pot, heat mascarpone over very low heat, stirring constantly, until warm and softened. Stir in sugar and amaretto and heat 1 to 2 minutes. Sprinkle cinnamon and nutmeg on top. Keep over low heat when serving.

COCONUT FONDUE

Try some fresh pineapple chunks as your dippers, for a piña colada flavor. Toasting the coconut in the oven will intensify the flavor.

2 tbs. cornstarch
1½ cups heavy cream
1 cup flaked coconut
½ cup coconut milk
½ cup sugar

Dissolve cornstarch in the cream in a fondue pot or saucepan and cook over medium heat, stirring constantly, until thickened. Add coconut, coconut milk and sugar and stir to mix well. Reduce heat to low and continue to cook, stirring, until sugar has dissolved. Keep over low heat when serving.

CRANBERRY RASPBERRY FONDUE

This tart fondue is best served with very sweet dippers, such as Almond Macaroons, *page 113, or frosted cookies and cakes. The cranberry flavor works well as a dessert for a holiday meal.*

1 tbs. cornstarch
$1/4$ cup water
1 can (16 oz.) cranberry sauce (jelly or whole berry)
$1/2$ cup framboise (raspberry liqueur)

Combine cornstarch and water in a small bowl; set aside. Melt cranberry sauce in a medium saucepan or fondue pot over medium-low heat, whisking frequently. Add framboise. When cranberry mixture begins to boil, add cornstarch mixture, whisking until fondue thickens. Keep over low heat when serving.

HOT BERRY FONDUE

You can use any combination of berries to create your own custom flavor. Fresh berries are always preferred, but unsweetened frozen berries, thawed, are just fine.

$1/2$ cup sugar
1 tablespoon cornstarch
2 cups raspberries, blackberries, strawberries or blueberries
2 tsp. freshly squeezed lemon juice
$1/3$ cup water

In a food processor workbowl or blender container, combine sugar and cornstarch. Add berries, lemon juice and water. Process until smooth. Pour into a fondue pot or saucepan and cook over medium heat until thickened. Keep over low heat when serving.

CHERRIES JUBILEE FONDUE

If you don't want the drama of flaming the brandy, you can stir it in before serving. If you opt for the dramatic flaming version, use caution, and the results will be spectacular.

2 cans (16 oz. each) cherry pie filling
$^3/_4$ cup apple juice, or more if needed
$^1/_4$ cup brandy

Place contents of 1 can of cherries into a blender container or food processor workbowl and process until very finely chopped. Add chopped cherries, the contents of the second can of cherries and apple juice to a fondue pot or saucepan and cook over medium heat until thickened. Add more apple juice if mixture is too thick.

Pour fondue into fondue pot if it was cooked in a saucepan. Take fondue away from heat source and pour brandy on top of fondue. Tilt pan slightly and, using a long match, carefully ignite brandy. Shake pan gently until the fire goes out. Stir briefly before serving. Keep over low heat when serving.

CHERRY CRANBERRY FONDUE

A nice change of pace for a holiday dessert, this fondue's bright red color is perfect for Christmas — and healthy to boot!

1 1/2 cups fresh whole cranberries
1 cup sugar
1/2 cup dried cherries, chopped
4 tsp. cornstarch
1 1/2 cups apple juice

Combine cranberries, sugar, cherries, cornstarch and apple juice in a saucepan or fondue pot. Cook over medium heat, stirring frequently, until mixture comes to a boil. Reduce heat to low and simmer for 10 minutes, until cranberries have all popped and mixture has thickened. Keep over low heat when serving.

MAPLE CHERRY FONDUE

A fun autumn fondue, it will remind you of waking up to a cold morning and warm waffles. In fact, cut-up waffle pieces are the perfect dipper for this fondue. This is very sweet, so try to keep the consistency on the thin side.

1½ cups maple syrup
1 cup light brown sugar, packed
2 tbs. butter
1⅓ cups minced dried cherries
½ cup heavy cream

In a medium saucepan or fondue pot, combine maple syrup, brown sugar and butter. Bring to a boil over medium heat, stirring frequently. Reduce heat to low, add cherries and simmer for 10 minutes. Remove from heat and stir in cream. Keep over low heat when serving.

LEMON FONDUE

Light and zesty, this is a fondue for spring and summer. Fresh strawberries are favorite dippers, as are gingerbread pieces and Mini Citrus Biscotti, *page 98.*

¹⁄₂ cup sugar
¹⁄₄ cup cornstarch
¹⁄₈ tsp. salt
2 cups water
¹⁄₄ cup (¹⁄₂ stick) butter
¹⁄₄ cup freshly squeezed lemon juice
1 heaping tbs. grated lemon zest

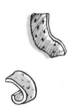

In a saucepan or fondue pot off heat, mix together sugar, cornstarch and salt. Stir in water until mixture is smooth. Bring to a boil over medium heat, stirring constantly, until thickened (about 2 minutes once mixture comes to a boil).

Remove from heat, add butter and stir until melted. Add lemon juice and zest and stir to mix. Keep over low heat when serving.

RUM RAISIN FONDUE

Curl up by the fire with this comforting fondue and chunks of gingerbread for dipping.

²/₃ cup raisins, coarsely chopped
½ cup dark rum
1 cup sugar
½ cup plus 2 tbs. water, divided

½ cup apple juice
4 tsp. cornstarch
2 tbs. butter

In a small bowl, combine raisins and rum. Set aside to soak for 15 minutes. In a heavy medium saucepan, combine sugar and ½ cup of the water. Bring to a boil over medium heat, stirring frequently. Reduce heat slightly and boil for 5 minutes. Stir in apple juice. In a small bowl, dissolve cornstarch in remaining 2 tablespoons water. Stirring constantly, add cornstarch and water to sugar mixture. Return mixture to a boil, stirring constantly. Stir in raisins with their soaking liquid and butter. Stir until butter has melted. Keep over low heat when serving.

CREAMY RUM RAISIN FONDUE

Remember rum raisin frozen custard? Here's the perfect version for cold nights.

$^3/_4$ cup water
1 cup sugar
$^1/_4$ cup ($^1/_2$ stick) butter
$^1/_2$ cup spiced rum
1 cup raisins, coarsely chopped
$^1/_2$ cup heavy cream

In a medium saucepan or fondue pot, combine water, sugar, butter, rum and raisins. Bring to a boil over medium heat, stirring frequently. Reduce heat slightly and boil for 5 minutes. Stir in cream, reduce heat to low and simmer for 10 minutes. Keep over low heat when serving.

APRICOT CREAM FONDUE

You can also used canned peaches if you prefer, for a peaches-and-cream fondue.

1 can (30 oz.) unpeeled apricot halves, drained
$1/3$ cup sugar
1 tbs. cornstarch
$3/4$ cup heavy cream
1 tbs. brandy or apricot brandy

Place apricots in a blender container and blend until smooth. In a medium saucepan or fondue pot, combine sugar and cornstarch. Stir in pureed apricots and cream. Cook over medium heat, stirring, until thickened and bubbly. Add brandy. Keep over low heat when serving.

ORANGE MARMALADE FONDUE

I like to use fresh pineapple as a dipper for this. Put bowls of shredded coconut out, to dip in after the fondue.

3 tbs. butter
3 tbs. light brown sugar
2 tsp. cornstarch
$1/2$ cup heavy cream
$1/3$ cup good quality orange marmalade
$1/2$ tsp. grated orange zest
2 tbs. orange liqueur, optional

In a fondue pot or small saucepan, melt butter over low heat. In a small bowl, combine brown sugar and cornstarch. Add to butter in saucepan and stir to combine. Stir in cream and cook over low heat until very thick. Remove from heat and add marmalade, grated zest and liqueur. Keep over low heat when serving.

ORANGE CREAM FONDUE

Based upon the taste of a Creamsicle, this fondue works well with tropical fruit dippers, or vanilla cakes and cookies.

1 cup heavy cream
1 cup half-and-half
$2/3$ cup sugar
4 egg yolks
zest from 2 large oranges

In a fondue pot or saucepan, heat cream, half-and-half and sugar over medium-low heat until very warm, but not boiling. In a small bowl, beat egg yolks. Pour a few spoonfuls of hot cream mixture into yolks and whisk thoroughly to temper. Pour yolk mixture into remaining hot cream mixture, whisking constantly, and return to heat. Cook mixture over medium heat until it coats the back of a wooden spoon, about 1 minute, being careful not to boil. Blend in orange zest. Keep over low heat when serving.

PINEAPPLE FONDUE

Serve this for dessert after a meal of Chinese takeout!

1 can (8 oz.) crushed pineapple in juice, not drained
1 can (6 oz.) unsweetened pineapple juice
$\frac{1}{4}$ cup light brown sugar, packed
2 tbs. cornstarch
$\frac{1}{4}$ cup water

In a saucepan or fondue pot, combine crushed pineapple (with its liquid), pineapple juice and sugar. Cook over medium heat until mixture comes to a boil. In a small bowl, dissolve cornstarch in water. Stir into hot pineapple mixture and continue to cook until thickened, about 2 minutes. Keep over low heat when serving.

DIPPERS

There are two critical things, besides flavors, to keep in mind when selecting your dippers: size and texture. You don't want any dipper larger than a single bite, so that the fondue will coat the dipper in a single dip. And if the texture is too crumbly, your fondue will be filled with bits of the dippers. Cut-up cakes are frequently used, but try to limit the amount of these items, and stick to cakes that won't fall apart easily, such as pound cake or angel food cake.

Serve tiny individual cookies and cakes when you can. For example, instead of making a pan of brownies and cutting them up, try making brownies in a mini muffin tin.

Many varieties of fruit make great dippers. In addition to the obvious (strawberries, bananas), try fresh pineapple, pear wedges, or fat, juicy blackberries. Dried fruit is also delicious with fondue, and has the added bonus of holding together very well. Dried apricots and chocolate fondue are a classic combination.

For the best dessert fondue, try some of the dipper recipes in this section. All are designed expressly for fondue, and in single-bite servings. And most can be made well in advance, making party preparations even easier.

SUGAR COOKIE BITES

Fast to mix and bake, these bite-sized cookies are perfect for most chocolate fondues. Be sure to keep the cookies small for easy dipping.

$^3/_4$ cup sugar

$^2/_3$ cup vegetable oil

2 tsp. vanilla extract

$^1/_2$ tsp. salt

2 eggs

2 tsp. baking powder

2 cups flour

Heat oven to 400°. In a large bowl, combine sugar, oil, vanilla, salt and eggs. Stir to mix well. In a separate bowl, stir together baking powder and flour. Add to sugar mixture and stir to form a dough. Drop by teaspoonfuls onto an ungreased cookie sheet. Using the bottom of a glass, press cookies down to about $^1/_4$-inch thick. Bake for 8 to 10 minutes, until light brown. Remove cookies to a rack to cool.

GINGER MOLASSES COOKIES

Makes about 60 cookies

Sweet and spicy, these are perfect for Pumpkin Fondue, *page 54, or* Lemon Fondue, *page 75, and are delicious on their own.*

3/4 cup (1 1/2 sticks) butter, softened
1 cup brown sugar, packed
1/4 cup molasses
1 egg
2 1/4 cups flour

2 tsp. baking soda
1 tsp. cinnamon
1 tsp. ground ginger
1/2 tsp. ground cloves
1/4 tsp. salt

In a large bowl, combine butter, brown sugar, molasses and egg until smooth. Stir in flour, baking soda, cinnamon, ginger, cloves and salt. Cover and refrigerate for at least 2 hours.

Heat oven to 375°. Lightly grease a cookie sheet. Shape dough into small balls, about 3/4-inch in diameter, and place on prepared cookie sheet. Bake for 8 to 10 minutes, or until just set but not hard. Remove cookies to a wire rack to cool.

CHERRY OATMEAL COOKIES

I love the taste of dried cherries and chocolate, so I really enjoy these cookies with many chocolate fondues.

$1\frac{1}{4}$ cups ($2\frac{1}{2}$ sticks) butter, softened
$1\frac{1}{4}$ cups light brown sugar, packed
1 egg
1 tsp. vanilla extract
$1\frac{1}{2}$ cups flour

1 tsp. baking soda
1 tsp. salt
3 cups quick-cooking oats
1 cup dried cherries, chopped

Heat oven to 375°. In a large bowl, using a mixer, beat together butter and brown sugar until light and fluffy. Beat in egg and vanilla. In a separate bowl, combine flour, baking soda and salt; add to creamed butter mixture, mixing well. Stir in oats and dried cherries. Drop by heaping teaspoonfuls onto an ungreased cookie sheet. Bake for 7 to 9 minutes or until light golden. Cool 1 minute on cookie sheet, then remove to a wire rack to cool completely.

COCONUT COOKIES

You can toast the coconut in the oven before adding to the dough to enhance the flavor.

3½ cups flour

2 cups sugar

2 cups (4 sticks) butter, softened

1 tbs. baking powder

1 tsp. baking soda

1 tsp. vanilla extract

1 cup flaked coconut

In a large bowl, combine flour, sugar, butter, baking powder, baking soda and vanilla. Beat at low speed using a mixer, scraping bowl often, until well mixed, about 3 to 4 minutes. Stir in coconut. Divide dough into quarters; shape each quarter into a 12 x 1-inch roll. Wrap in waxed paper or plastic wrap. Refrigerate until firm, at least 2 hours.

Heat oven to 350°. Cut rolls into ¼-inch slices. Place onto ungreased cookie sheets. Bake for 7 to 11 minutes, or until edges are lightly browned. Cool briefly on cookie sheets and then remove to a wire rack to cool completely.

VANILLA CHIP COOKIES

Makes about 60 cookies

Simple vanilla cookies are the perfect accompaniment to just about any fondue.

$^1/_2$ cup (1 stick) butter, softened
$^1/_2$ cup granulated sugar
$^1/_4$ cup light brown sugar, packed
1 tsp. vanilla extract
1 egg

1 cup flour
$^1/_4$ tsp. salt
$^1/_2$ tsp. baking soda
1 cup white chocolate baking chips
$^1/_2$ cup flaked coconut, optional

Heat oven to 375°. In a large bowl, using a mixer, beat butter until light. Gradually add sugars, beating until fluffy. Beat in vanilla and egg. In a separate bowl, stir together flour, salt and baking soda. Add flour mixture to butter mixture, blending well. Stir in white chocolate and coconut, if using. Drop by rounded teaspoonfuls onto ungreased cookie sheets. Bake for 7 to 9 minutes or until golden. Remove to wire racks to cool.

NUT COOKIES

Walnuts, peanuts and almonds are my favorite nuts to use, but feel free to use your favorites — try hazelnuts, macadamias, even Brazil nuts.

$2/3$ cup butter, softened
$1^{1}/_{3}$ cups light brown sugar, packed
2 eggs
$1^{1}/_{2}$ tsp. vanilla extract

$1^{2}/_{3}$ cups flour
$1/2$ tsp. baking soda
$1/2$ tsp. salt
2 cups finely chopped nuts

Grease 2 cookie sheets. Heat oven to 350°. In a large bowl, using a mixer, beat together butter and sugar. Beat in eggs and vanilla until light and fluffy. In a separate bowl, combine flour, baking soda and salt; gradually add to creamed mixture. Fold in nuts. Drop by teaspoonfuls 2 inches apart on prepared cookie sheets. Bake for 10 to 12 minutes or until browned and almost set (centers will be soft). Remove to a wire rack to cool.

MACADAMIA NUT BITES

These cookies offer a surprise — a big macadamia nut in the center!

$1/2$ cup (1 stick) butter, softened
$1/2$ cup sugar
1 egg
1 tbs.vanilla extract
$1 1/2$ cups flour
$1/8$ tsp. salt
1 can (5 oz.) whole macadamia nuts

Heat oven to 350°. In a large bowl, using a mixer on low speed, beat butter and sugar until blended. Increase speed to medium-high and beat until fluffy. Beat in egg and vanilla. Stir in flour and salt. Shape 1 teaspoonful of dough around each macadamia nut. Place on ungreased cookie sheets. Bake for 10 to 13 minutes or until golden around base of each cookie. Remove to wire racks to cool.

MOCHA CHIP COOKIES

Since these cookies have a strong coffee-chocolate flavor, they are best used with simple chocolate or vanilla fondues.

$^1/_2$ cup granulated sugar
$^1/_2$ cup brown sugar, packed
$^1/_2$ cup (1 stick) butter, softened
1 egg
$1^1/_2$ cups flour

2 tbs. instant coffee granules
1 tsp. baking soda
$^1/_4$ tsp. salt
2 cups mini chocolate chips or mini M&Ms

Heat oven to 350°. In a large bowl, using a mixer on medium speed, cream together granulated sugar, brown sugar and butter until light and fluffy. Add egg and beat until smooth. Stir in flour, instant coffee, baking soda and salt. Stir in chocolate chips. Drop by teaspoonfuls onto an ungreased cookie sheet. Bake for 8 to 10 minutes until golden brown. Remove to a wire rack to cool.

FUDGY NUTTY COOKIES

Dense chocolate and lots of nuts make this chewy cookie irresistible.

2 cups (12 oz.) chocolate chips
2 tbs. butter
3/4 cup flour
2 tsp. vanilla extract
1 can (14 oz.) sweetened condensed milk
2 cups chopped pecans or walnuts

Heat oven to 350°. Line a cookie sheet with foil and grease foil lightly. In a microwave-safe bowl, combine chocolate and butter. Heat on high power 1 to 2 minutes, stirring every 30 seconds, until just melted and smooth. Stir in flour until well blended. Add vanilla and condensed milk and mix well. Stir in nuts. Drop dough by level tablespoonfuls onto foil about 2 inches apart. Bake for 8 to 9 minutes (cookies will be soft on top) . Cool on cookie sheet for 2 minutes. Lift foil from cookie sheet and place onto rack to cool. When cool, carefully remove cookies from foil.

CHEWY CHOCOLATE CINNAMON COOKIES

If you like the taste of Mexican Chocolate Fondue, *page 11, you'll love these cookies.*

6 tbs. (³/₄ stick) butter, softened
²/₃ cup light brown sugar, packed
¹/₄ cup granulated sugar
1 egg
1 tsp. baking soda
¹/₄ cup light corn syrup
1 tsp. vanilla extract
1¹/₂ cups flour
¹/₃ cup unsweetened cocoa powder
¹/₂ tsp. cinnamon

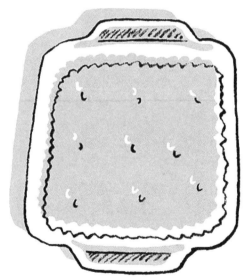

In a large bowl, using a mixer, beat together butter, brown sugar and granulated sugar until light and fluffy. Add egg, baking soda, corn syrup and vanilla. Mix well. In a separate bowl, stir together flour, cocoa powder and cinnamon and add to butter mixture. Mix well. Cover dough and refrigerate for at least 1 hour.

Heat oven to 350°. Shape dough into small balls, about $3/4$ to 1 inch in diameter. Bake for 9 to 10 minutes, or until cookies are set and tops are cracked. Cool on cookie sheet for a few minutes. Remove to a wire rack to cool completely.

BROWNIE COOKIES

Brownies are great to dip in fondue, but cut brownies will leave crumbs in your pot. Try these chewy brownie cookies; each one is a perfect bite.

$2/3$ cup butter, softened
$1^1/_2$ cups light brown sugar, packed
1 tbs. water
1 tsp. vanilla extract
2 eggs
$1^1/_2$ cups flour
$1/_3$ cup unsweetened cocoa powder
$1^1/_2$ tsp. baking soda
$1/_2$ tsp. salt
2 cups (12 oz.) semisweet chocolate chips

Heat oven to 375°. In a large bowl, using a mixer, beat together butter, brown sugar, water and vanilla. Add eggs and beat well.

In a separate bowl, combine flour, cocoa powder, baking soda and salt. Beat into creamed mixture at low speed until just blended. Stir in chocolate chips. Drop by rounded tablespoonfuls 2 inches apart onto an ungreased cookie sheet. Bake for 7 to 9 minutes.

Cookies will appear slightly underbaked. Cool on cookie sheet for 2 minutes. Remove to a wire rack to cool completely.

MINI CITRUS BISCOTTI

Smaller than store-bought biscotti, these work much better for fondue. You can make these lemon or orange flavored, depending on your preference. Both are delicious.

$^2/_3$ cup sugar
$^1/_2$ cup vegetable oil
1 tbs. grated orange or lemon zest
1 tsp. vanilla extract
2 eggs
$2^1/_2$ cups flour
1 tsp. baking powder
$^1/_4$ tsp. baking soda
$^1/_4$ tsp. salt

Heat oven to 350°. In a large bowl, using a mixer, beat together sugar, oil, zest, vanilla and eggs. Stir in flour, baking powder, baking soda and salt. Dough will be stiff. Shape into 4 logs, about 10 inches long by 1½ inches wide each, on an ungreased cookie sheet. Bake for 15 to 20 minutes, until a toothpick inserted in center comes out clean. Remove from oven

and cool for 15 minutes. Leave oven at 350°. Cut logs crosswise into ½-inch slices. Place cookies cut side down onto cookie sheet. Return to oven and bake for 10 minutes, until lightly browned. Cool cookies on a wire rack.

NUTTY BISCOTTI

These biscotti are not as hard as traditional biscotti, so they can easily be skewered for fondues.

$2/3$ cup butter, softened
$1\frac{1}{2}$ cups sugar
4 eggs
1 tbs. vanilla extract
$4\frac{1}{2}$ cups flour
1 tbs. baking powder
$1/2$ tsp. salt
1 cup chopped pecans

Heat oven to 325°. Grease and flour 2 cookie sheets. In a large bowl, using a mixer, beat together butter and sugar until light and fluffy. Beat in eggs and vanilla until well mixed. Stir in flour, baking powder, salt and pecans. Dough will be stiff. Divide dough into 4 equal portions. Shape each portion into a log about 12 inches long. Place 2 logs onto each prepared cookie sheet, about 2 inches apart. Bake for 25 to 30 minutes, or until logs are just beginning to brown.

Remove logs from oven and cool on cookie sheets for 10 minutes. Leave oven at 325°. Slice logs diagonally about $1/2$-inch thick. Place slices, cut side down, on cookie sheets and return to oven. Bake slices for 5 minutes, turn cookies over and bake an additional 5 minutes, or until golden. Remove cookies to a wire rack to cool.

MADELEINES

You will need a special madeleine pan to make these classic cookies. Although they are a bit larger than bite-sized, they taste so good in many fondues that I had to include the recipe.

$^3/_4$ cup (1$^1/_2$ sticks) butter
1 tbs. vegetable oil
2 eggs
$^3/_4$ cup sugar
$^1/_2$ tsp. vanilla extract
1 cup flour

Heat oven to 425°. Prepare a madeleine pan by spraying with nonstick spray. Set aside. In a small saucepan over low heat, melt butter with the oil. Set aside to cool slightly. In a large bowl, using a mixer on low speed, beat together eggs, sugar and vanilla until blended. Increase speed to high and beat until thick and very light colored, about 5 minutes. Reduce speed to medium and add in butter mixture until blended. Using a wire whisk, gently stir in flour. Spoon about 1 tablespoon of batter into each madeleine shell. Bake for 8 to 10 minutes, until golden. Immediately remove cookies from shells to a rack to cool.

CHOCOLATE BISCOTTI BITES

Makes about 60 biscotti

Seriously chocolate, these little cookies are wonderful in many fondues.

$^1/_2$ cup (1 stick) butter, softened
$1^1/_4$ cups sugar
2 eggs
1 tsp. vanilla extract

$2^1/_4$ cups flour
$^1/_4$ cup unsweetened cocoa powder
1 tsp. baking powder
$^1/_4$ tsp. salt

Heat oven to 350°. In a large bowl, using a mixer, beat together butter and sugar until light and fluffy. Add eggs and vanilla and mix well. In a separate bowl, stir together flour, cocoa powder, baking powder and salt. Add to butter mixture, beating until smooth. Dough will be stiff. Shape into 4 logs, about 10 inches long by $1^1/_2$ inches wide each, on an ungreased cookie sheet. Bake for 20 minutes.

Remove from oven and cool for 15 minutes. Leave oven at 350°. Cut logs crosswise into $^1/_2$-inch slices. Place cookies cut side down onto cookie sheet. Return to oven and bake for another 8 minutes. Remove cookies to a wire rack to cool.

BUTTERY SHORTBREAD

Store-bought shortbread tends to be dry and fragile. This recipe still produces a buttery cookie, but one that won't break apart quite as easily.

2$\frac{1}{4}$ cups flour
$\frac{1}{4}$ tsp. baking powder
$\frac{1}{4}$ tsp. salt
$\frac{1}{2}$ cup confectioner's sugar
1 cup (2 sticks) plus 2 tbs. butter, softened
1$\frac{1}{4}$ tsp. vanilla extract

Heat oven to 350°. In a medium bowl, stir together flour, baking powder, salt and confectioner's sugar. Stir in butter and vanilla until a stiff dough forms. Pat dough into an ungreased 9-inch square baking pan and prick well with a fork. Bake for 35 to 40 minutes, until edges turn golden. Cut into bite-sized squares while warm. Cool on wire rack; separate cookies.

BROWN SUGAR SHORTBREAD

Makes about 48 cookies

These can get crunchy, so be sure to make them the same day you plan on serving them, or store them in an airtight container as soon as they've cooled completely.

1 cup (2 sticks) butter, softened
1¼ cups brown sugar, packed
1 tsp. vanilla extract
2½ cups flour

In a large bowl, using a mixer, beat together butter and brown sugar until creamy. Add vanilla and then gradually add flour, beating well. Gather dough into a ball and wrap tightly in plastic wrap. Refrigerate until firm, at least 2 hours.

Heat oven to 300°. Lightly grease a cookie sheet. On a lightly floured board, roll out dough to ¼-inch thick. Cut with cookie cutters into small shapes and place onto prepared cookie sheet. Bake for 25 to 30 minutes, until centers are almost firm. Cool cookies on cookie sheet.

BRANDY BALLS

Brandy and nuts flavor these little cookies and are a great item to include with your holiday fondues. Using flavoring instead of real brandy makes these cookies more kid-friendly.

1¼ cups (2½ sticks) butter, softened
½ cup sugar
1 egg yolk
2 tsp. brandy flavoring

3 cups flour
¼ tsp. salt
1 cup finely chopped walnuts or pecans

Heat oven to 350°. Lightly grease a cookie sheet. In a large bowl, using a mixer, beat together butter and sugar until light and fluffy. Beat in egg yolk and brandy flavoring. In a separate bowl, stir together flour and salt. Add flour mixture to butter mixture, stirring to combine well. Stir in nuts until well combined. Roll dough into 1-inch balls and place on prepared cookie sheet. Bake for about 25 minutes, or until firm to touch and very light golden. Remove cookies to a rack to cool.

SOUR CREAM POUND CAKE

Makes 1 loaf

Dense and rich, this cake cuts up very well into cubes for dipping.

$1/2$ cup (1 stick) butter, softened
3 eggs
$1/2$ cup sour cream
$1^1/2$ cups flour
$1/4$ tsp. baking powder
$1/8$ tsp. baking soda
1 cup sugar
$3/4$ tsp. vanilla extract

Heat oven to 325°. Leave butter, eggs and sour cream at room temperature for 30 minutes. Grease and lightly flour a 9 x 5-inch loaf pan. In a small bowl, stir together flour, baking powder and baking soda; set aside. In a large bowl beat butter with a mixer on medium speed for 30 seconds. Gradually add sugar, beating about 10 minutes or until very light and fluffy. Beat in vanilla. Add eggs, 1 at a time, beating for 1 minute after each addition. Add flour mixture and sour cream alternately to beaten mixture, beating on low speed after each addition just until combined. Pour batter into prepared pan, spreading evenly. Bake for 60 to 75 minutes or till a wooden toothpick inserted in the center comes out clean. Cool in pan on a wire rack for 10 minutes. Remove cake from pan; cool on rack completely before cutting into cubes.

CREAM CHEESE BITES

Makes about 36 cookies

These sweet little cookies have a chewy texture with a cream cheese tang. Great with chocolate or fruit fondues.

1/2 cup (1 stick) butter, softened
4 oz. cream cheese, softened
1 cup sugar
1 tsp. vanilla extract
1 cup flour

Heat oven to 350°. In a large bowl, using a mixer, beat together butter, cream cheese and sugar until creamy. Beat in vanilla. Gradually add in flour, mixing thoroughly. Drop by rounded teaspoonfuls onto an ungreased cookie sheet. Bake for 10 to 12 minutes, or until edges are golden. Remove cookies to a wire rack to cool.

ULTIMATE KRISPIE TREATS

Makes about 60 dippers

Rice Krispie Treats are great dippers. They don't dissolve or break apart and can be cut into tiny bites. My version below starts with the basic recipe, but adds white chocolate chips and nuts for a treat that adults will fall in love with.

1/4 cup (1/2 stick) butter
40 regular marshmallows, or 4 cups miniature marshmallows
1 tsp. vanilla extract
6 cups Rice Krispies® cereal
2 cups white chocolate baking chips
1 cup chopped macadamia nuts or pecans

Butter a cookie sheet. In a large microwave-safe bowl, melt butter and marshmallows on high power for 3 minutes, stirring after 2 minutes. Stir mixture until smooth. Add vanilla. Add cereal, white chocolate chips and nuts. Stir until well combined. Spoon mixture onto prepared cookie sheet, pressing down evenly to about 1 inch thick. Cool completely before cutting into 1-inch squares.

MINI CREAM PUFFS

If you have a pastry bag, you can fill the puffs with a sweet custard or whipped cream just before serving, for a decadent dipper. Unfilled, these puffs are still a sophisticated dipper and a nice change of pace from cakes and cookies.

$1/2$ cup (1 stick) butter
1 cup water
$1/4$ tsp. salt

1 cup flour
4 eggs

Heat oven to 375°. Grease 2 large cookie sheets and set aside. In a large saucepan over medium heat, heat butter, water and salt until butter is melted and mixture boils. Remove from heat. Add flour all at once and with a wooden spoon stir vigorously until mixture forms a ball and leaves sides of pan. Add eggs to flour mixture 1 at a time, beating well after each egg until smooth. Using a spoon and spatula, drop batter onto prepared cookie sheets in small, bite-size mounds. Bake for 20 to 30 minutes, until golden. Remove cream puffs to a wire rack to cool.

ALMOND MACAROONS

Sweet and nutty, these complement chocolate fondues well.

2 cups blanched almonds
3/4 cup sugar
2 tsp. almond extract
2 egg whites, at room temperature

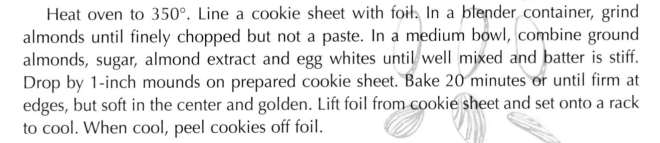

Heat oven to 350°. Line a cookie sheet with foil. In a blender container, grind almonds until finely chopped but not a paste. In a medium bowl, combine ground almonds, sugar, almond extract and egg whites until well mixed and batter is stiff. Drop by 1-inch mounds on prepared cookie sheet. Bake 20 minutes or until firm at edges, but soft in the center and golden. Lift foil from cookie sheet and set onto a rack to cool. When cool, peel cookies off foil.

WALNUT BREAD

Studded with nuts, this dense bread cuts well and dips even better.

3 cups flour

1$\frac{1}{2}$ cups chopped walnuts

5 tsp. baking powder

1$\frac{1}{4}$ cups sugar

1$\frac{1}{2}$ tsp. salt

3 eggs

1$\frac{1}{2}$ cups milk

$\frac{1}{3}$ cup vegetable oil

Heat oven to 350°. Grease a 9 x 5-inch loaf pan. In a large bowl, mix together flour, nuts, baking powder, sugar and salt. In a separate bowl, beat together eggs, milk and oil. Pour into flour mixture and stir until just combined. Pour batter into prepared pan and bake for about 80 minutes, until a toothpick inserted in the center comes out clean. Remove from oven and cool on rack for 10 minutes. Remove from pan and cool completely before cutting.

HONEY CAKE

Sweet and dense, this cake cuts very well into cubes for dipping.

1 cup (2 sticks) butter, softened
1 cup honey
4 eggs
3 cups flour
2 tsp. baking powder
$\frac{1}{2}$ tsp. salt
1 cup chopped walnuts, optional

Heat oven to 350°. Grease a 9 x 5-inch loaf pan. In a large bowl, using a mixer, beat together butter with honey. Add eggs and beat well. In a medium bowl, stir together flour, baking powder and salt. Add flour mixture to honey mixture along with walnuts, if using, and stir only until combined. Pour into prepared loaf pan and bake for about 1 hour, or until a toothpick inserted in the center comes out clean. Remove to a rack to cool completely before cutting.

CRISPY KNOTS

Although these are crisp, the shape makes them easy to spear with your fondue fork. Their neutral flavor can be used with any fondue recipe.

2 eggs
1/4 cup sugar
2 1/2 tbs. brandy
2 1/2 tbs. butter, softened
1/4 tsp. salt
2 cups flour, divided
vegetable oil, for frying

In a large bowl, using a mixer, beat together eggs and sugar until thick and lemon-colored. Add brandy, butter and salt and mix well. Stir in 1 1/2 cups of the flour. Spread remaining flour out onto a board or countertop. Turn dough out onto the floured board and knead until smooth. Wrap in plastic wrap and set aside to rest at room temperature for 30 minutes.

Work with ⅓ of dough at a time. On a well-floured board, roll out each portion to a 6 x 30-inch rectangle. Dough will be very thin. Cut into 1 x 6-inch strips. Tie each strip into a loose knot.

In a large, deep skillet over medium heat, pour oil to a depth of 1 inch. Heat oil until it reaches 360° on a thermometer. Add a few cookies and cook, turning once, until golden brown all over. Remove cookies to a paper towel to drain. Continue with remaining cookies.

BLONDIES

Also known as butterscotch brownies, these chewy bites are full of brown sugar flavor.

1/4 cup (1/2 stick) butter, softened
1 cup light brown sugar, packed
1 egg
1 tsp. vanilla extract
1 cup flour
1 tsp. baking powder
1/2 tsp. salt

Heat oven to 375°. Grease an 8-inch square baking pan. In a large bowl, using a mixer, beat together butter with brown sugar until light and fluffy. Add egg and vanilla and stir until well mixed. Stir in flour, baking powder and salt. Spread batter into prepared pan. Bake for 20 to 25 minutes, or until golden brown. Cool completely in pan and then cut into small squares.

BANANA BARS

If you love the pairing of chocolate and bananas, these bar cookies will be a great addition to your next fondue party, dipped into chocolate fondue.

6 tbs. (³/₄ stick) butter, softened
1 cup brown sugar, packed
1 egg
¹/₂ tsp. vanilla extract

1 large, very ripe banana, mashed
1³/₄ cups flour
1¹/₂ tsp. baking powder
¹/₂ tsp. salt

Heat oven to 350°. Grease a 9-inch-square baking pan. In a large bowl, using a mixer, beat together butter and sugar until light and fluffy. Add egg, vanilla and banana and mix well. In a separate bowl, stir together flour, baking powder and salt. Add to butter mixture and stir just to combine. Spread batter into prepared pan. Bake for 35 to 40 minutes, or until golden brown. Cool in pan before cutting into small squares.

INDEX

Serve Creative, Easy, Nutritious Meals with **nitty gritty**® Cookbooks

1 or 2, Cooking for
100 Dynamite Desserts
9 x 13 Pan Cookbook
Asian Cooking
Bagels, Best
Barbecue Cookbook
Beer and Good Food
Big Book Bread Machine
Big Book Kitchen Appliance
Big Book Snack, Appetizer
Blender Drinks
Bread Baking
New Bread Machine Book
Bread Machine III
Bread Machine V
Bread Machine VI
Bread Machine, Entrees
Burger Bible
Cappuccino/Espresso
Casseroles
Chicken, Unbeatable
Chile Peppers
Cooking in Clay

Coffee and Tea
Convection Oven
Cook-Ahead Cookbook
Crockery Pot, Extra-Special
Deep Fryer
Dehydrator Cookbook
Dessert Fondues
Edible Gifts
Edible Pockets
Fabulous Fiber Cookery
Fondue and Hot Dips
Fondue, New International
Freezer, 'Fridge, Pantry
Garlic Cookbook
Grains, Cooking with
Healthy Cooking on Run
Ice Cream Maker
Indoor Grill, Cooking on
Irish Pub Cooking
Italian, Quick and Easy
Juicer Book II
Kids, Cooking with Your
Kids, Healthy Snacks for

Loaf Pan, Recipes for
Low-Carb
No Salt No Sugar No Fat
Party Foods/Appetizers
Pasta Machine Cookbook
Pasta, Quick and Easy
Pinch of Time
Pizza, Best
Porcelain, Cooking in
Pressure Cooker
Rice Cooker
Salmon Cookbook
Sandwich Maker
Simple Substitutions
Slow Cooking
Slow Cooker, Vegetarian
Soups and Stews
Soy & Tofu Recipes
Tapas Fantásticas
Toaster Oven Cookbook
Waffles & Pizzelles
Wedding Catering book
Wraps and Roll-Ups

"Millions of books sold—for more than 35 years"   For a free catalog, call: Bristol Publishing Enterprises
(800) 346-4889
www.bristolpublishing.com